ED EMBERLEY'S GREAT THUMBPRINT DRAWING BOOK

SCHOLASTIC INC.
New York Toronto London Auckland Sydney

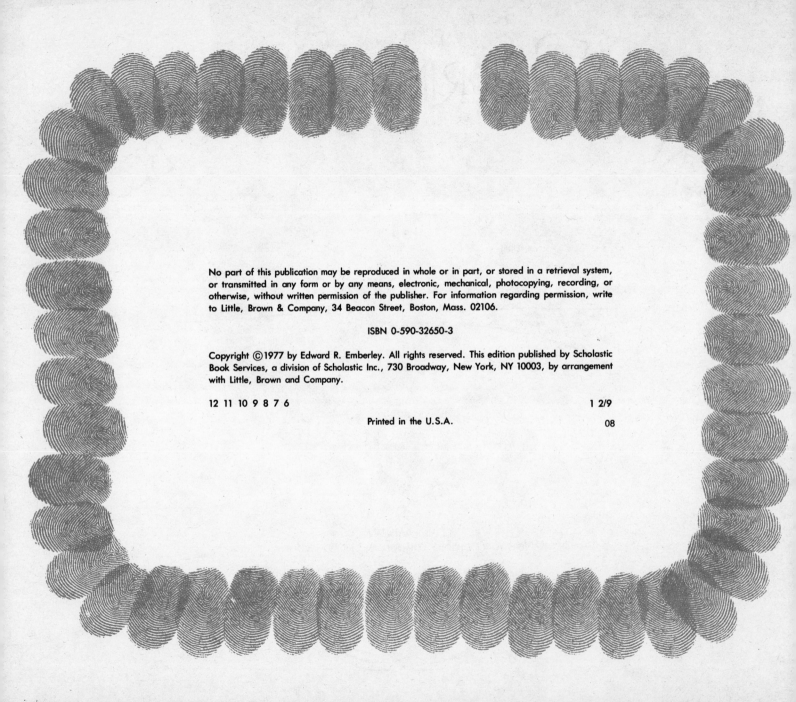

ISBN 0-590-32650-3

12 11 10 9 8 7 6   1 2/9

Printed in the U.S.A.   08

WHERE TO FIND IT PAGE

THIS BOOK SHOWS HOW TO DRAW PICTURES.
USING THIS NAME AND THUMBPRINTS.

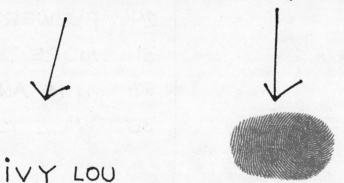

iVY LOU

FOR INSTANCE,
THESE LETTERS PLUS THIS PRINT MAKE THIS BIRD!

ᴜᴜᴜᴜ ᴠᴠᴠ · ıı + =

HERE'S HOW

THIS ROW SHOWS
<u>WHAT</u> TO DRAW.

THIS ROW SHOWS
<u>WHERE</u> TO PUT IT.

ALSO

THERE WILL BE: ↑
LETTERS TURNED AROUND,
SCRIBBLES,
AND FILLING IN.

(THIS SIGN MEANS FILL IN → 〰)

FOR INSTANCE

PERSON (MORE FOLKS ON PAGE 9)

(JUST A LINE CAN MAKE A HAT.)

..   U   II   II   --   —

WALKING (MORE ACTION ON PAGE 15)

..   U   ∧   /\   ∨∕   —

5

FISH (MORE CRITTERS ON PAGE 20)

·   ∪   ∪∪ ⋒   ⊂⊂   ⊂⊂⊂⊂⊂

BIRD (MORE BIRDS ON PAGE 24)

·   <   ᴐᴐ   ∪∪ || ><

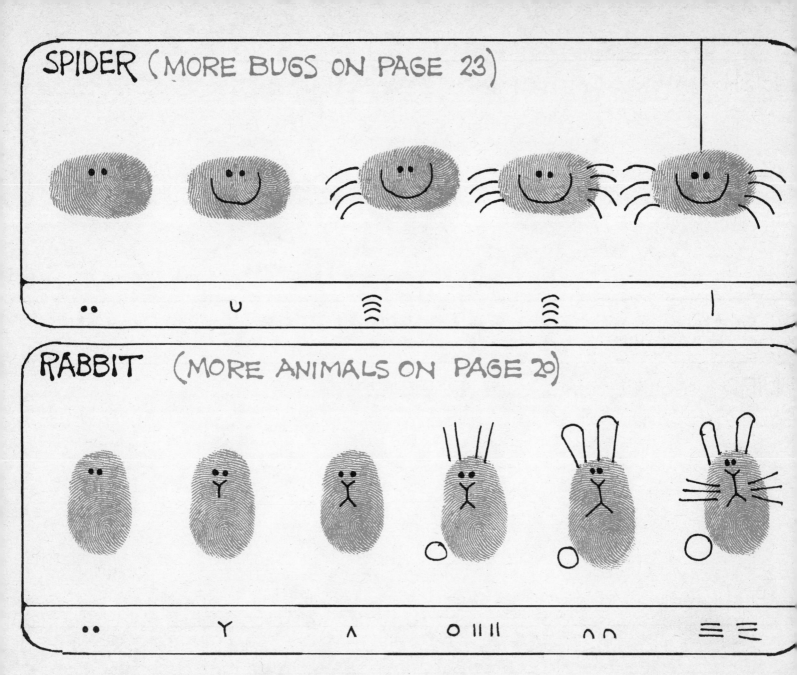

SPIDER (MORE BUGS ON PAGE 23)

RABBIT (MORE ANIMALS ON PAGE 20)

HALLOWEEN (MORE HOLIDAYS ON PAGE 26)

_ ∧   ∧∧   ∧   - - -   ∪ ⋏⋏⋏∪

FROG (MORE THINGS WITH 2 THUMBPRINTS ON PAGE 31)

∩∩   ∪   ●●‥ |||| ∪∪∪∪

8

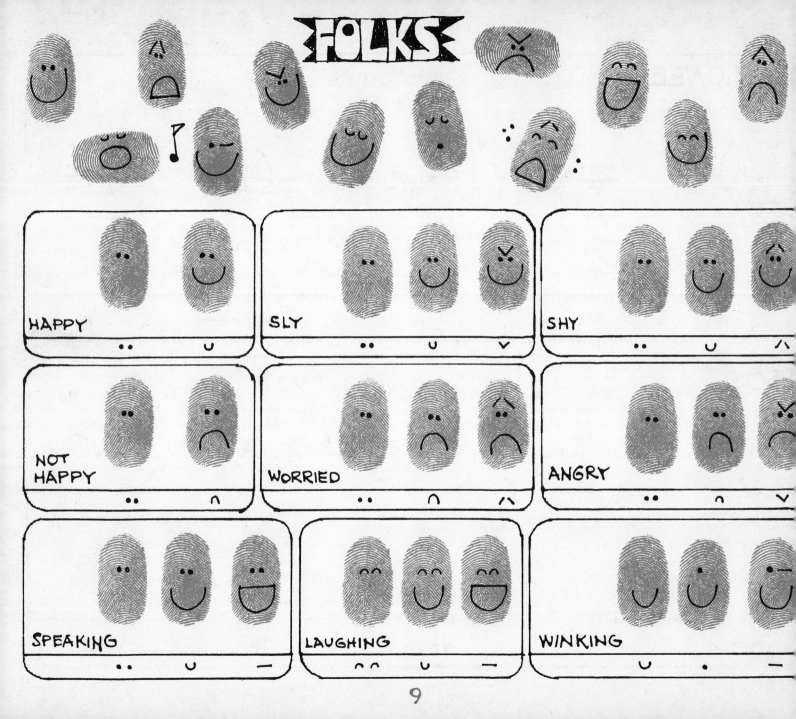

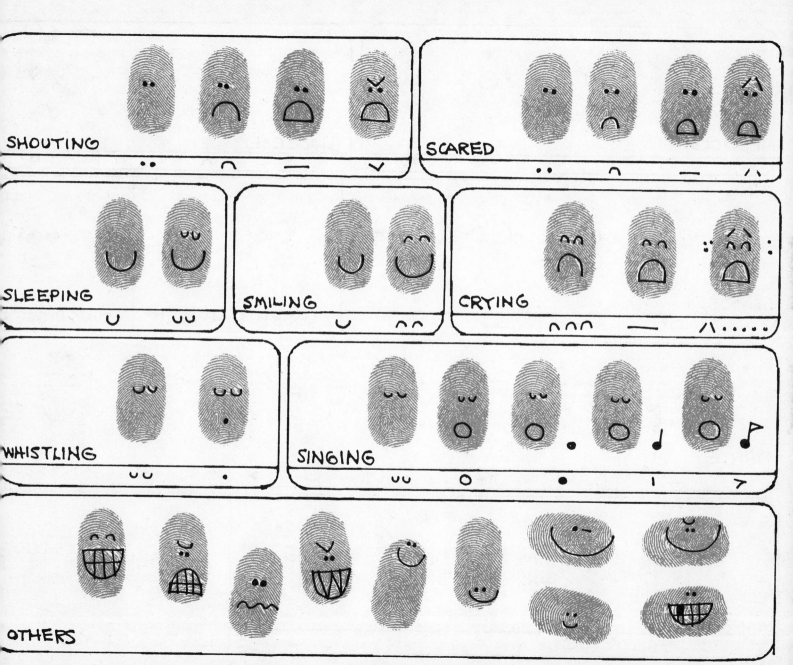

SHOUTING

SCARED

SLEEPING

SMILING

CRYING

WHISTLING

SINGING

OTHERS

10

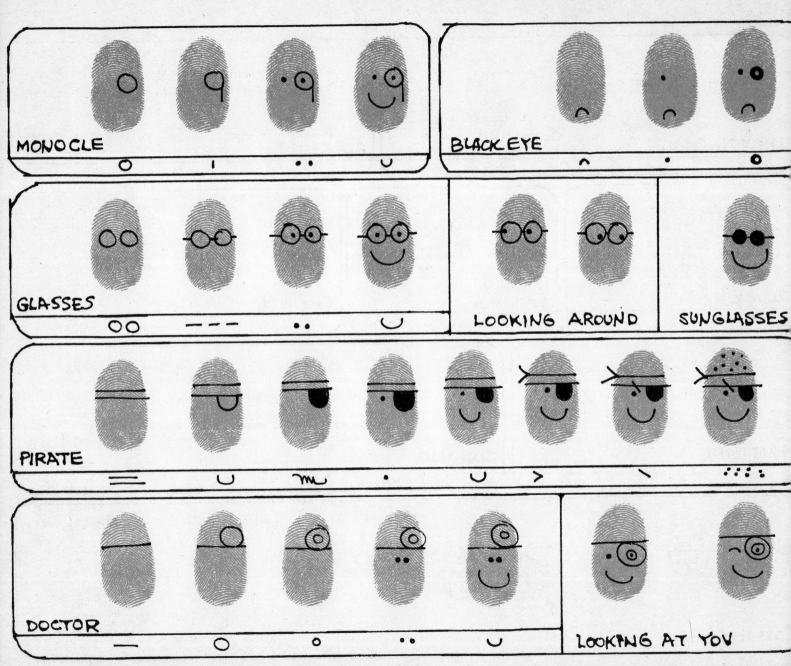

MONOCLE

BLACK EYE

GLASSES

LOOKING AROUND

SUNGLASSES

PIRATE

DOCTOR

LOOKING AT YOU

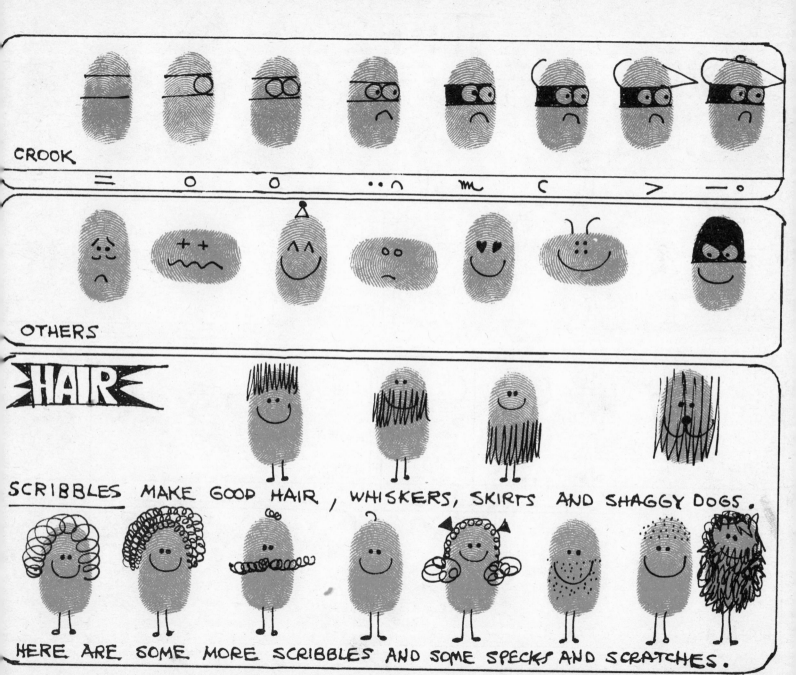

CROOK

$=$ o o $\cdot\cdot\cap$ m $($ $>$ $-o$

OTHERS

HAIR

SCRIBBLES MAKE GOOD HAIR, WHISKERS, SKIRTS AND SHAGGY DOGS.

HERE ARE SOME MORE SCRIBBLES AND SOME SPECKS AND SCRATCHES.

12

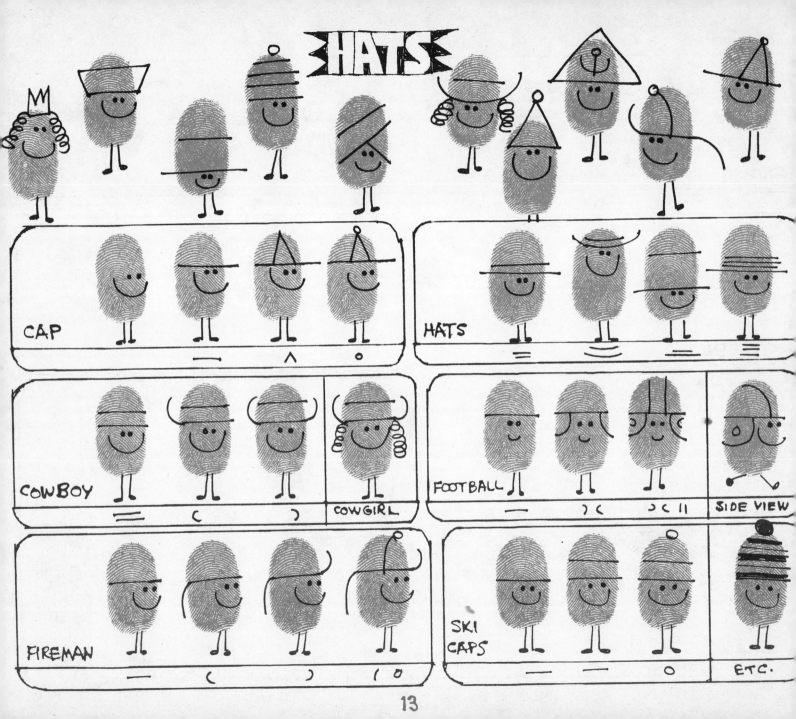

HATS

CAP

HATS

COWBOY

COWGIRL

FOOTBALL

SIDE VIEW

FIREMAN

SKI CAPS

ETC.

13

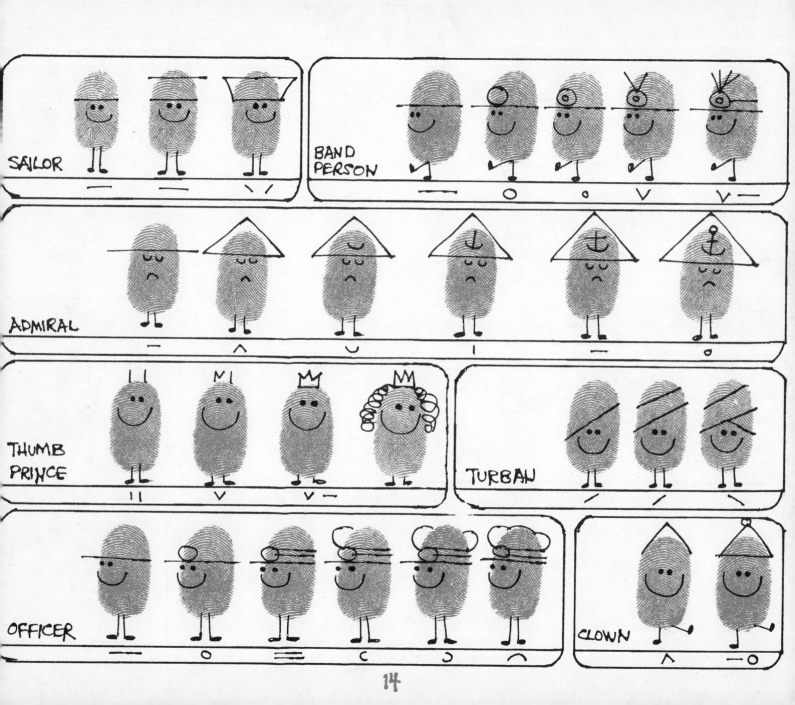

SAILOR

BAND PERSON

ADMIRAL

THUMB PRINCE

TURBAN

OFFICER

CLOWN

14

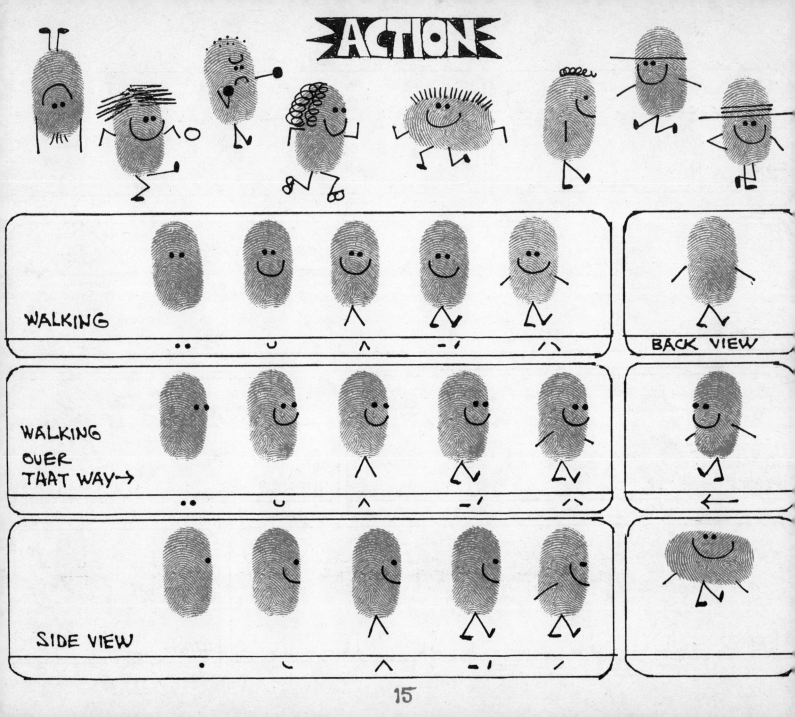

ACTION

WALKING

BACK VIEW

WALKING OVER THAT WAY→

SIDE VIEW

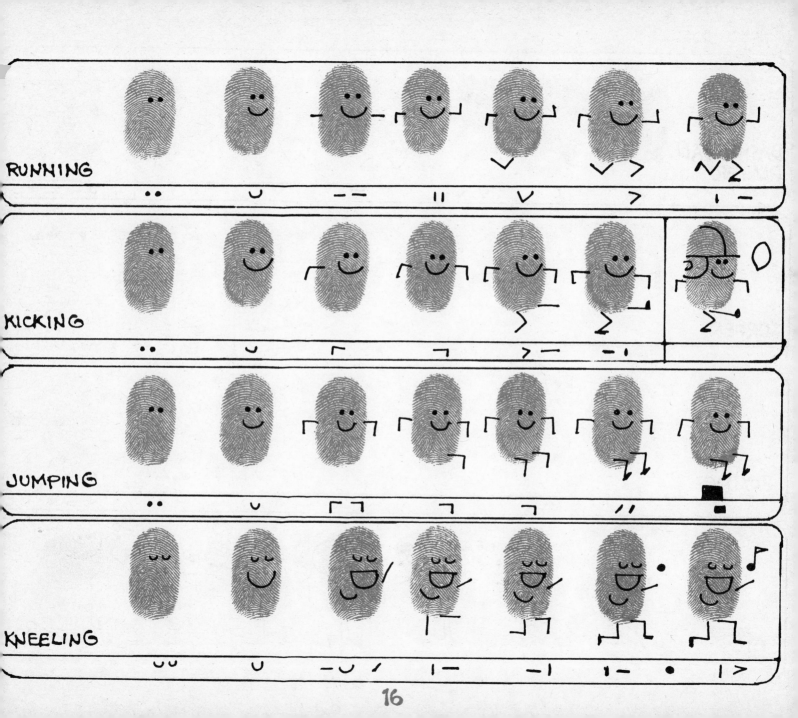

RUNNING

KICKING

JUMPING

KNEELING

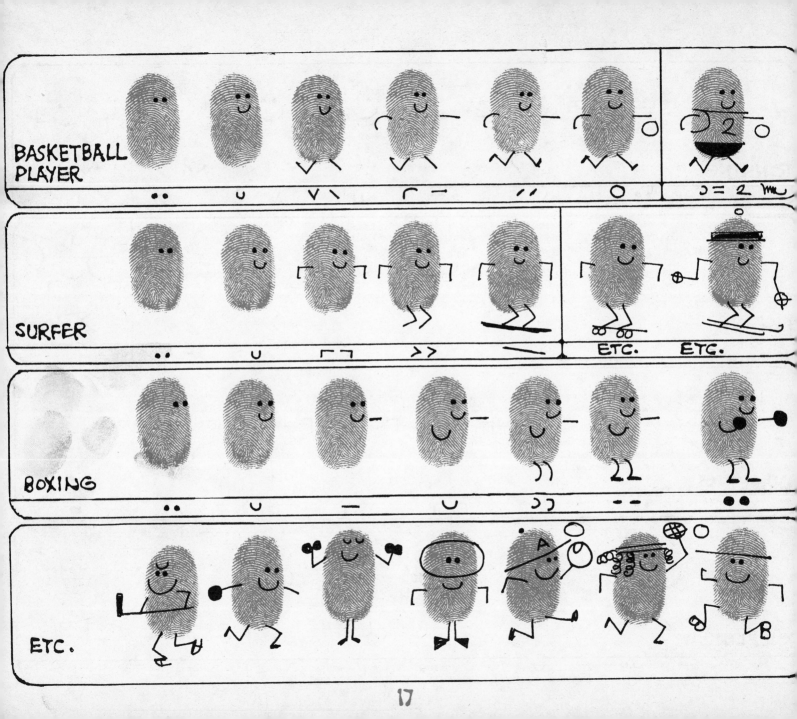

BASKETBALL PLAYER

SURFER

ETC.　　ETC.

BOXING

ETC.

17

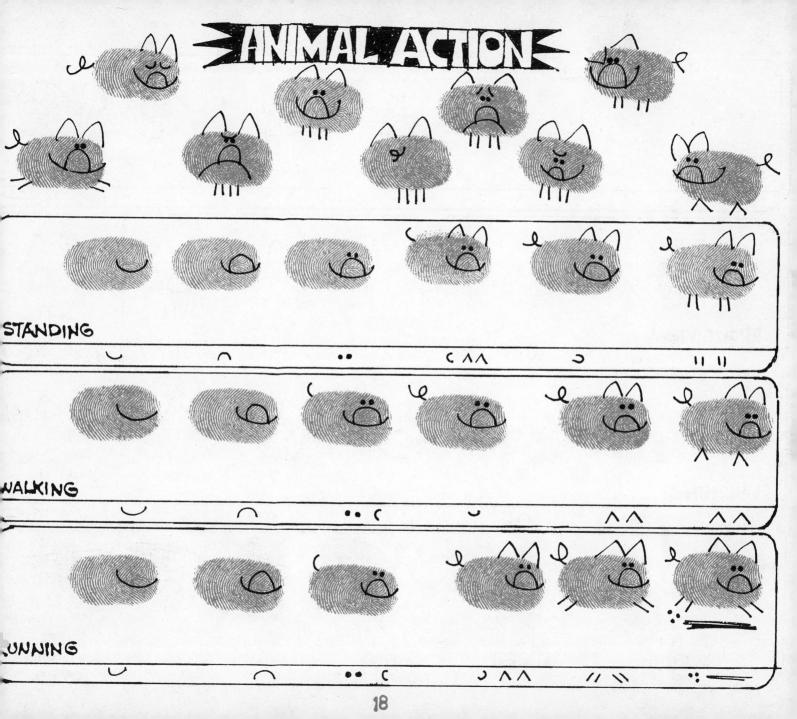

ANIMAL ACTION

STANDING

WALKING

RUNNING

18

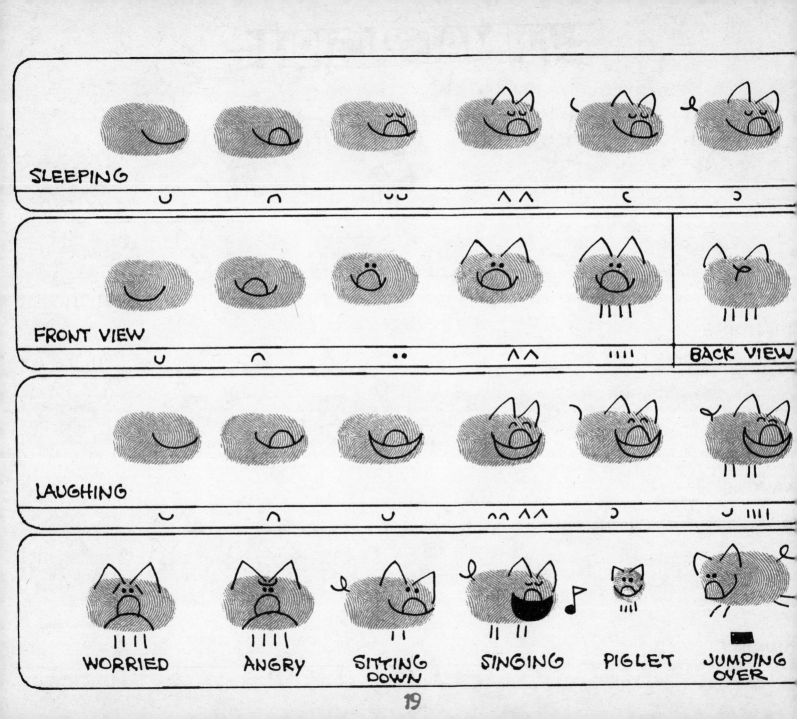

SLEEPING

FRONT VIEW

BACK VIEW

LAUGHING

WORRIED   ANGRY   SITTING DOWN   SINGING   PIGLET   JUMPING OVER

19

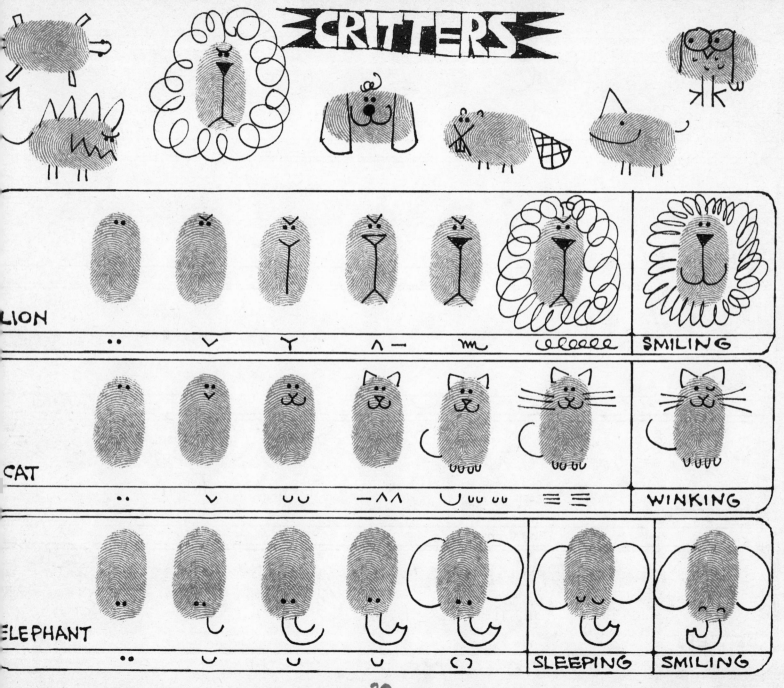

CRITTERS

| LION | .. | ∨ | Y | ∧ — | ⋙ | eeeee | SMILING |

| CAT | .. | ∨ | ∪∪ | —∧∧ | ∪ ∪∪ ∪∪ | ≡ ≡ | WINKING |

| ELEPHANT | .. | ∪ | ∪ | ∪ | ( ) | SLEEPING | SMILING |

20

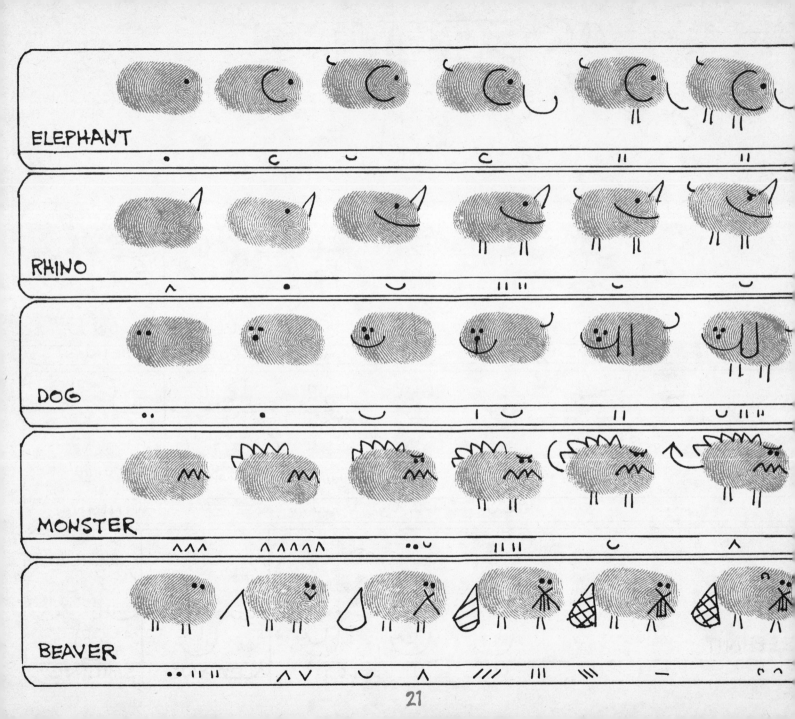

ELEPHANT

RHINO

DOG

MONSTER

BEAVER

21

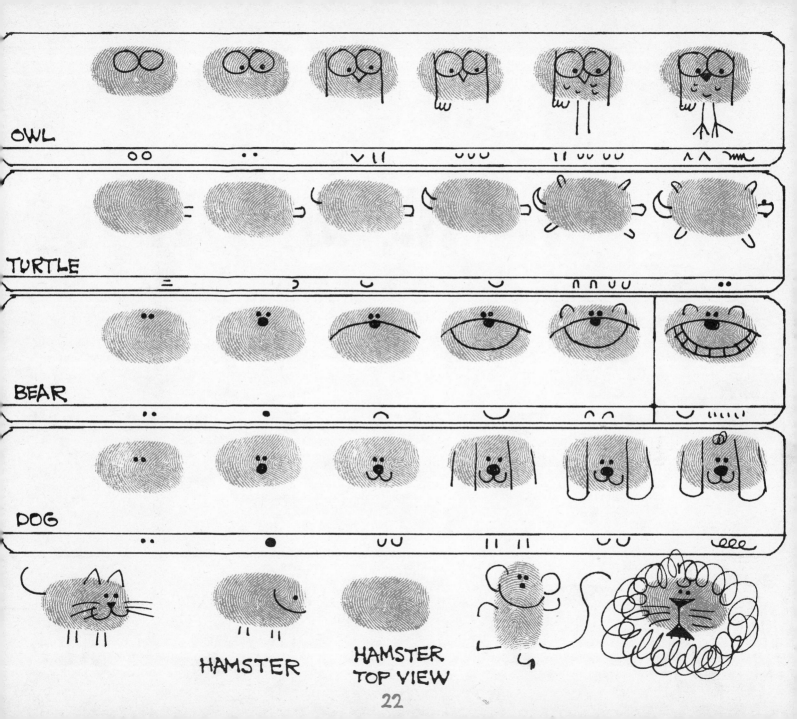

OWL

TURTLE

BEAR

DOG

HAMSTER

HAMSTER TOP VIEW

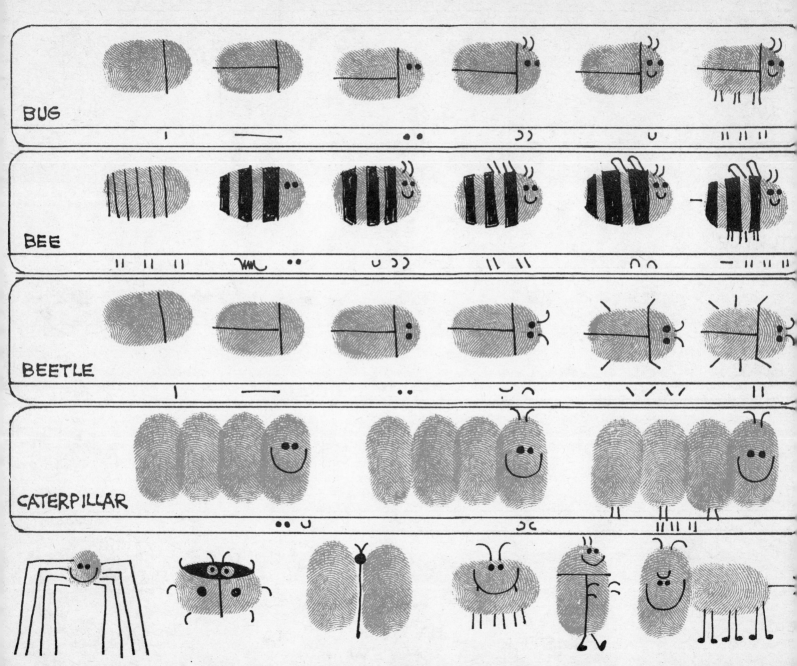

BUG

BEE

BEETLE

CATERPILLAR

23

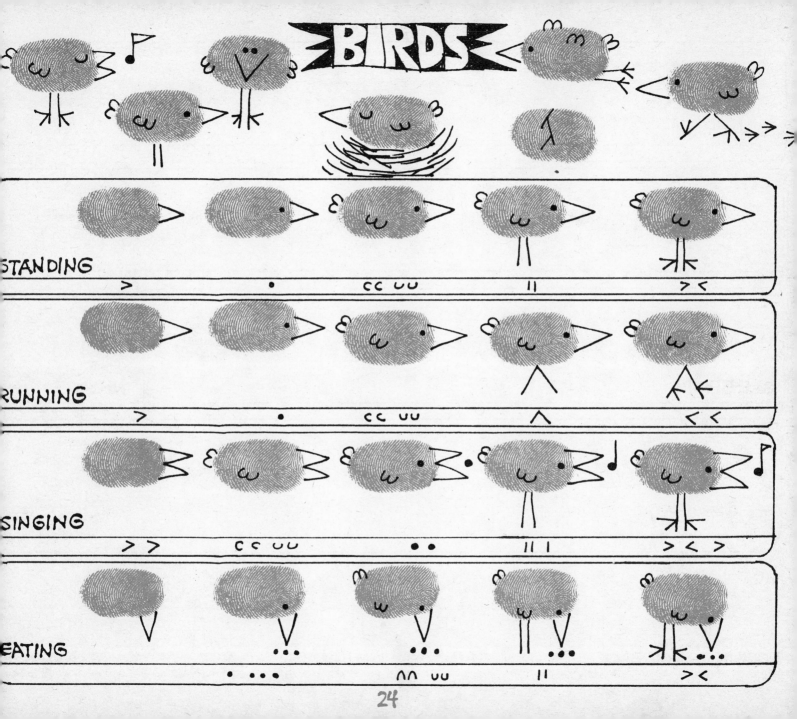

BIRDS

STANDING

RUNNING

SINGING

EATING

24

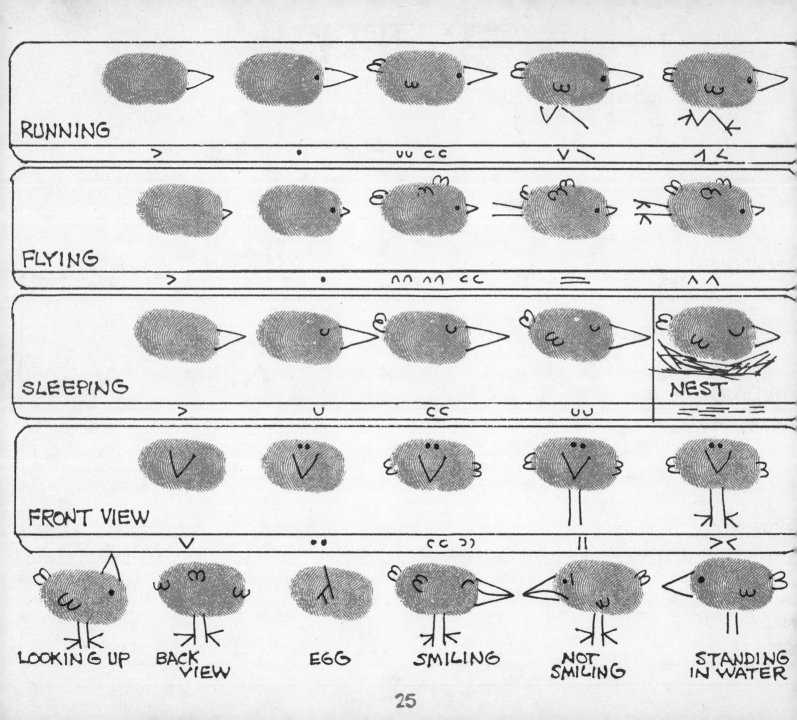

RUNNING

FLYING

SLEEPING   NEST

FRONT VIEW

LOOKING UP   BACK VIEW   EGG   SMILING   NOT SMILING   STANDING IN WATER

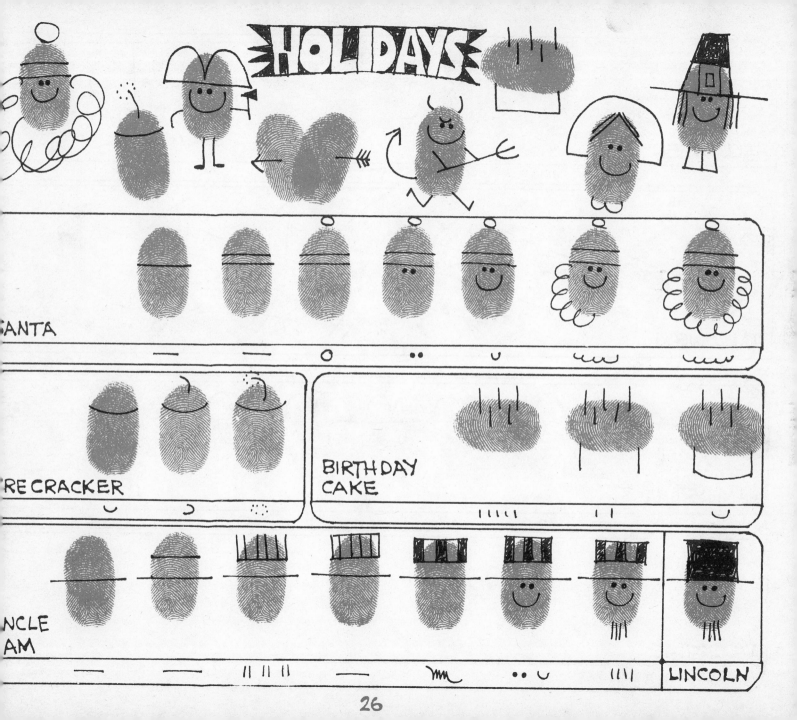

HOLIDAYS

SANTA

RE CRACKER

BIRTHDAY CAKE

NCLE AM

LINCOLN

26

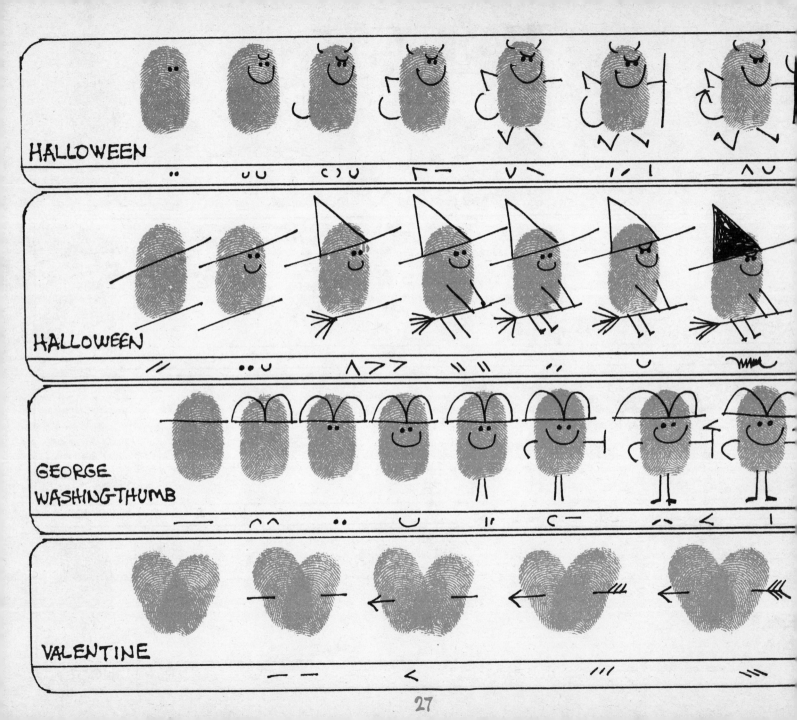

HALLOWEEN

HALLOWEEN

GEORGE
WASHINGTHUMB

VALENTINE

27

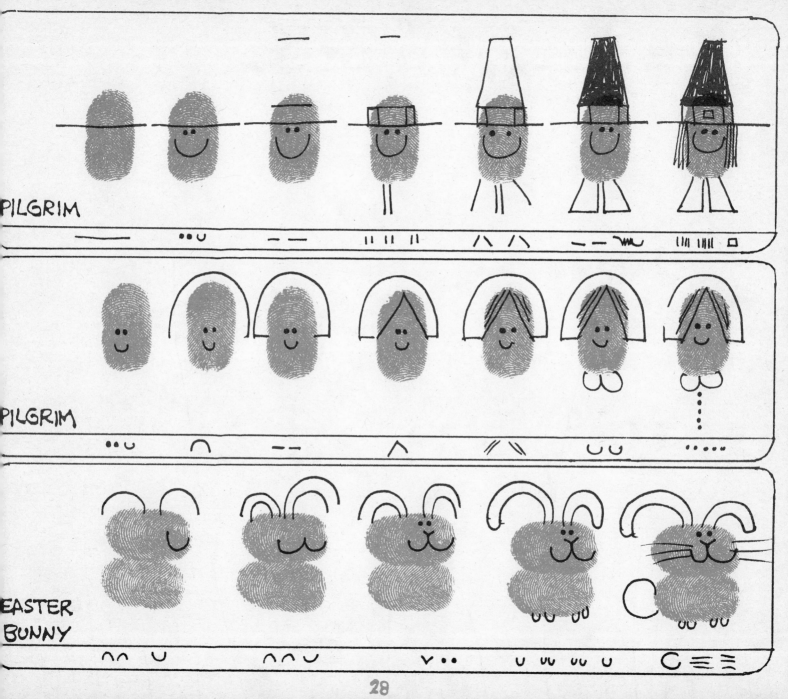

PILGRIM

PILGRIM

EASTER
BUNNY

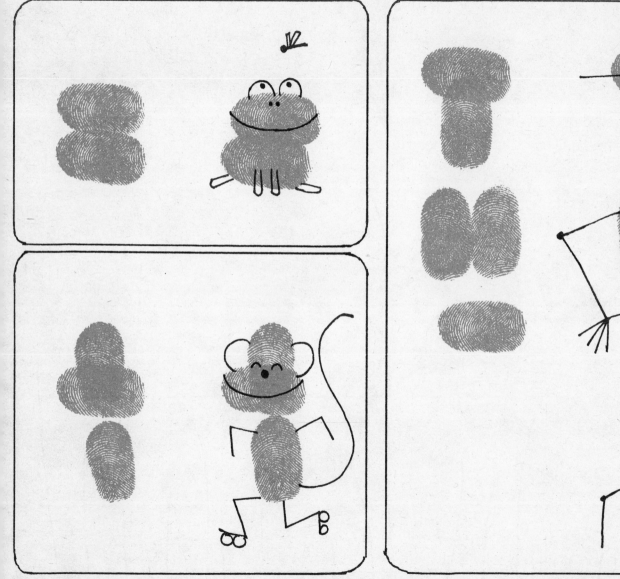

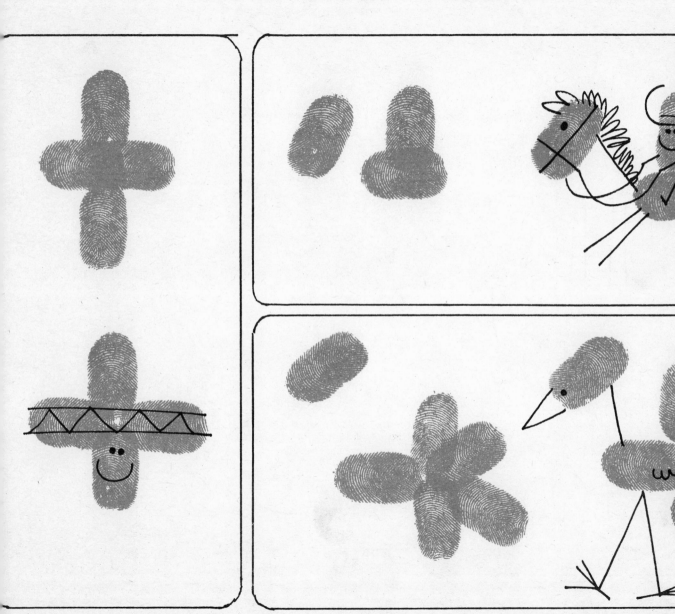

THIS AND THAT

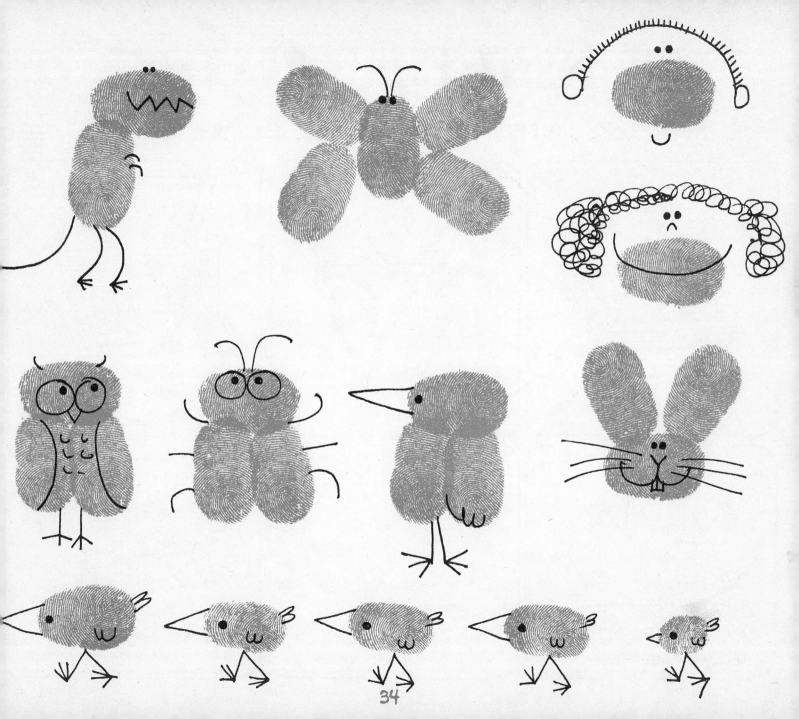

WAYS TO MAKE PRINTS

FOR THIS BOOK I USED A STAMP PAD I BOUGHT IN THE 5 AND 10

A METAL
BOX.

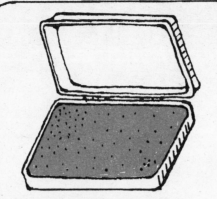

A DAMP,
INKY SPONGE
INSIDE.

I PRESSED
MY THUMB ON
THE PAD.

THEN I PRESSED
MY THUMB ON
THE PAPER —

I LET THE
PRINT DRY —

THEN I
DREW ON IT.

YOU CAN PAINT YOUR THUMB WITH WATER COLOR OR POSTER PAINT AND STAMP IT.

POSTER PAINT

YOU CAN MAKE YOUR OWN PAD FROM A SPONGE OR A FOLDED CLOTH SOAKED WITH FROSTING COLOR.

YOU CAN USE A CUT CARROT OR POTATO.

CUT   PAINT   STAMP   DRY   DRAW

YOU CAN DRAW A ROUND SHAPE OR MAKE A BLOB.

BLOB   ROUND SHAPE   PAINTED THUMB   STAMP PAD   CARROT   POTATO

- THERE ARE MORE THAN
  4 BILLION THUMBS
  IN THIS WORLD.
- NO TWO THUMBPRINTS
  HAVE <u>EVER</u> BEEN FOUND
  THAT ARE JUST ALIKE.
- THAT MEANS THAT THERE
  IS NO OTHER THUMBPRINT
  IN THIS WORLD EXACTLY LIKE YOURS.
- I THINK THAT MAKES YOUR THUMBPRINT SOMETHING SPECIAL!

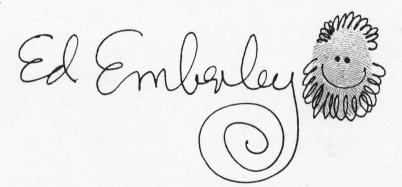

Ed Emberley